Sand Swimmers

The Secret Life of Australia's Desert Wilderness

Narelle Oliver

CANDLEWICK PRESS

In the center of Australia lies a strange desert wilderness.

There are huge waves, not of water, but of fiery red sand.
There are lakes of glittering salt and rivers of cracking clay.
Spiky grass grows in circles, like giant sea urchins.
Scorching plains of polished stones stretch out forever
like a shimmering ocean.

At first glance, nothing moves.
It is hard to believe that anything could live in this harsh place.

It has not always been like this.
In times long past, this land was cooler and there was plenty of rain.

Wildlife of Central Australia in the middle Miocene epoch (14–16 million years ago),
left to right: giant flightless dromornithid bird, diprotodontid, rhabdosteid river dolphin,
quinkanine crocodile, dragonfly

Large marsupials called diprotodontids, as big as cows, roamed the forests.
And dolphins played in lakes that were never dry.

6

As millions of years passed, the rain fell less often.
It became hotter. Many plants and animals died.

Theropod dinosaur
footprints

Opalized platypus jaw

Seabed ripples,
jellyfish imprint

Horned turtle fossils

Now, the only memories of that lush playground are some
rare fossils, as well as small pockets of rain-forest animals
and plants clinging to life in shady, spring-fed gorges.

Green tree frog

Rainbow bee-eater

Cabbage palms

Rainbow fish

Today, the center of Australia is mostly hot, dry desert.
Many call it the "Dead Heart," for that is what it seems to be.

But the Dead Heart has a secret life.

Some Aboriginal peoples have known
about this secret life for thousands of years.

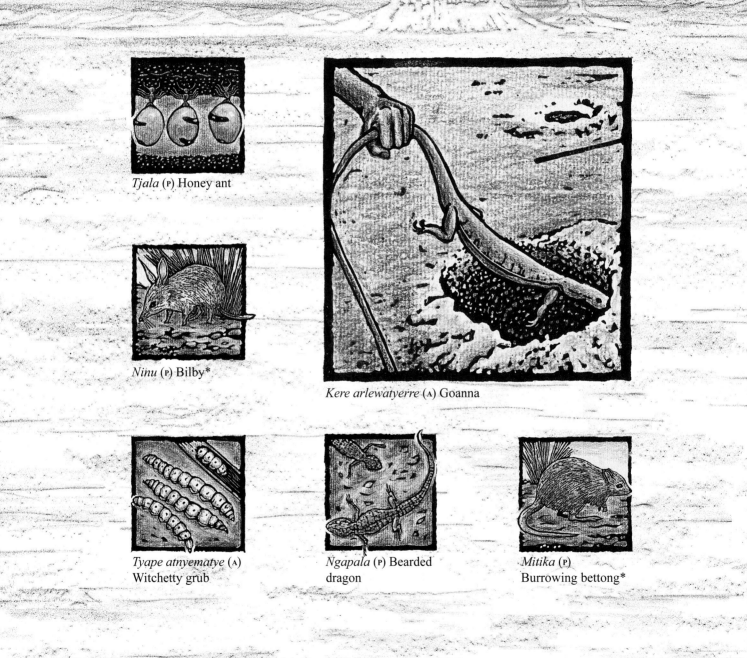

Tjala (ᴘ) Honey ant

Ninu (ᴘ) Bilby*

Kere arlewatyerre (ᴀ) Goanna

Tyape atnyematye (ᴀ)
Witchetty grub

Ngapala (ᴘ) Bearded
dragon

Mitika (ᴘ)
Burrowing bettong*

*Endangered since European settlement. Replaced by feral rabbits as food source
  for indigenous peoples.

To live in the desert, they had to discover
and understand its plants and hidden creatures.

Wakati (P) Portulaca seed for damper

Merne utyerrke (A)
Desert fig

Merne alangkwe (A)
Bush banana

Merne pmerlpe (A)
Quandong

Tjanpi (PIN)
Desert lemon grass

Merne anatye (A)
Bush potato

(P) Pitjantjatjara language   (A) Arrernte language   (PIN) Pintupi language

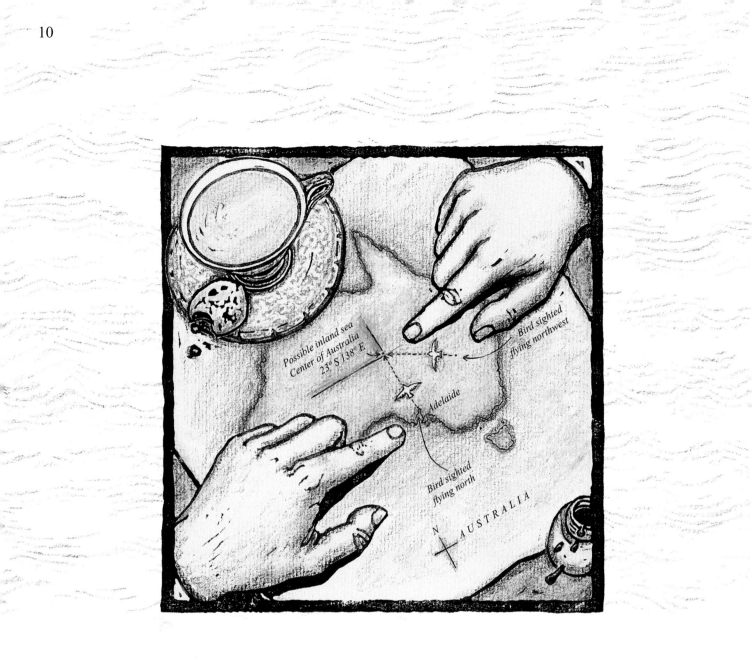

The first European explorers saw the center of
Australia with different eyes.

Page 3
Expedition to Centre of Australia
Departure: 10th August 1844

Requirements:
1 boat
5 carts
11 horses
30 bullocks
200 sheep

Assorted vegetable seedlings
melon seedlings

rifles
flag

Some, like Charles Sturt, dreamed of discovering
an inland sea, perhaps the lush forests and lakes of
ancient times. And to this land they hoped to bring
their own plants and animals.

Salt-lake ground-dragon

But the land those explorers found was nothing like their dreams. With each step, the country seemed drier and more hostile.

Not far into their journey, they came upon one of the most forbidding desert areas—a salt lake. Before them was blinding hot salt as far as the eye could see.

It was impossible to imagine any life in such a place.

"Not a living thing to be seen, not an ant, not a cricket, or a grasshopper."

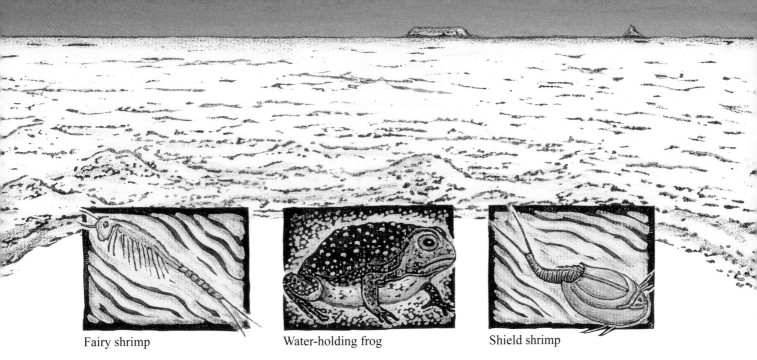

Fairy shrimp

Water-holding frog

Shield shrimp

But, like much of the Australian desert, these salt lakes have their surprises.

Disguised as a ripple of salt, the salt-lake ground-dragon slips from its winter hideout beneath the crust. Like a firewalker, it crosses the blistering surface in search of ants.

The salt crust is also home to millions of tiny eggs. When it rains, they change into masses of wriggling shrimp, which lay eggs of their own.

Where there is less salt, water-holding frogs burrow deep into the desert clay and make a waterproof cocoon, like plastic wrap. They will not emerge until heavy rains soak down deep enough to reach them. They often wait in hiding for years and years.

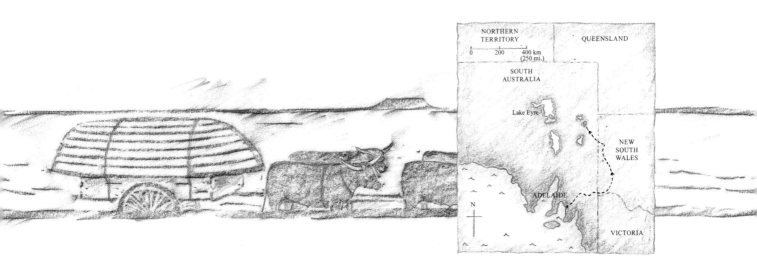

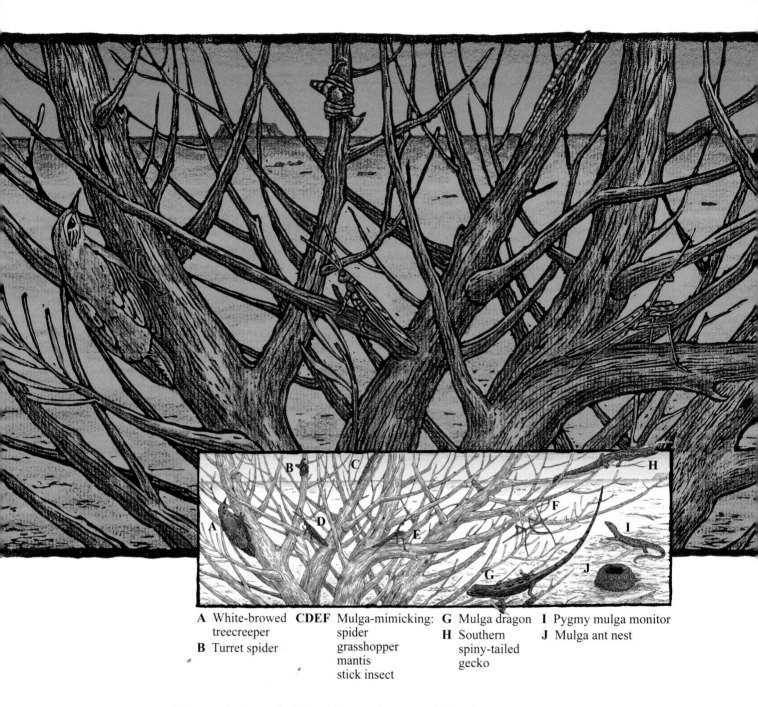

A White-browed treecreeper	**CDEF** Mulga-mimicking: spider grasshopper mantis stick insect	**G** Mulga dragon	**I** Pygmy mulga monitor	
B Turret spider		**H** Southern spiny-tailed gecko	**J** Mulga ant nest	

Beyond the salt lakes lie mulga scrublands—strange, wiry timber tangled so thickly in places that it is difficult to pass through.

"Did man ever see such a place? A kind of dread came over me as I gazed upon it."

Although it was a curse for those early explorers, the mulga provides a haven for a variety of desert creatures. There are shady hiding places in the trees and in leaf litter. Even when the mulga dwellers move around to feed, they seem to remain hidden.

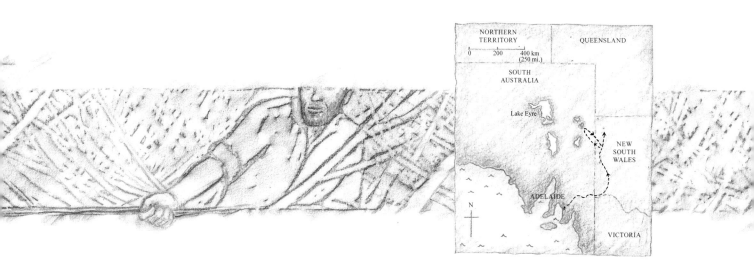

16

Mulgara Scorpion Honey ant Spinifex hopping-mouse Painted ground-dragon

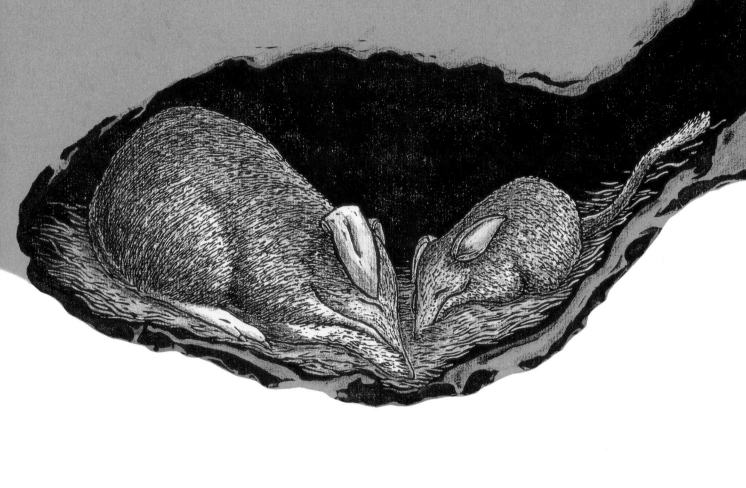

"So hot our hair, like sheep's wool, ceased to grow and our nails became brittle as glass."

Below the mulga scrublands and the open desert plains are the secret cities. Living underground is often the best way to escape the dry desert heat and hungry predators.

Honey ants gather nectar from the mulga and store it belowground in the bloated bodies of storage ants. In especially dry times, the ants feed from these living honey pots in their deep, dark cellars.

Bilbies and other mammals sleep in their cooler, moister burrows during the heat of the day, saving their energy for night hunting.

This idea was also used by Sturt's party. For six months of their expedition, it was too hot to keep going. So, like the unseen tunnel animals around them, the explorers dug an underground room. They sheltered there near a shrinking creek until the worst heat was over.

With only limited rations, a small party continued toward the center.

Still dreaming of an inland sea, they were shocked to find an ocean of burning stones. Polished by sandstorms and packed hard, the searing desert pavement stretched in every direction.

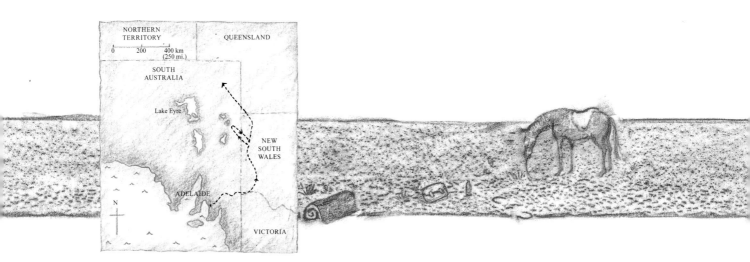

A Gibber-hopper
B Gibberbird
C Gibber earless dragon
D Inland dotterel
E Gibber gecko

Amazingly, some creatures have made this fiery furnace their home. Their bodies cope with intense heat, glare, and lack of water. To be safe on the bare, stony flats, they must be masters of disguise. And to complete their deception, they usually keep still.

"We steered our course over this dreary desert as a ship at sea."

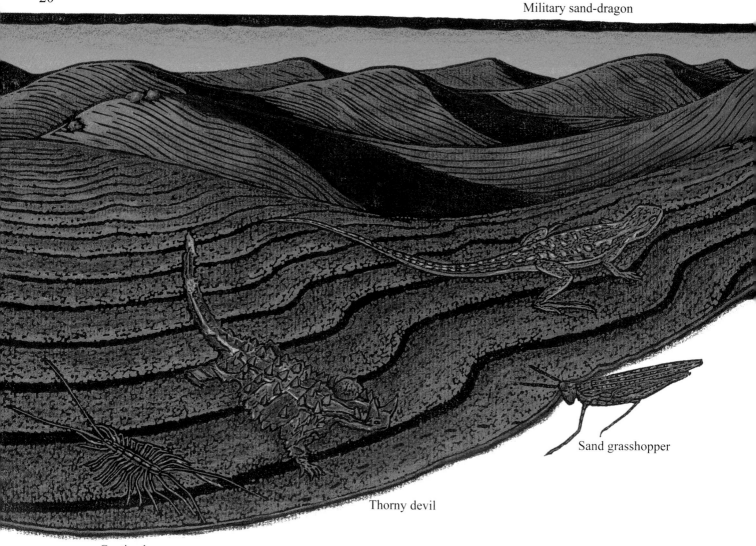

Sand grasshopper

Thorny devil

Centipede

After oceans of stones, Sturt's party came upon huge waves of sand that loomed above them row upon row like a stormy sea. Horrified by the endless dunes, Sturt declared this place to be as hot and desolate as the "entrance to Hell."

"Like gigantic ripples left by the tide in its ebb and flow."

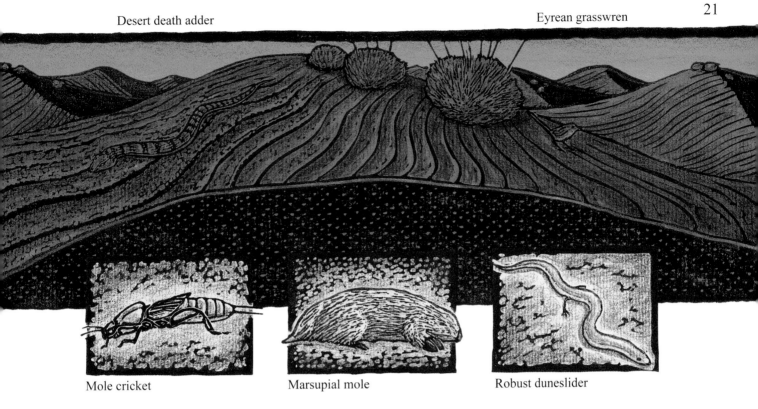

Mole cricket   Marsupial mole   Robust duneslider

Yet these desert sands are host to a remarkable secret society.

Almost invisible, sand-patterned animals slither, scuttle, or hop across the surface. The sand grasshopper conceals itself even more by half-submerging.

And like the sea, the sand waves also contain swimmers.

Often their only trace is a tiny moving ripple. They are busy hunting insects just below the surface. One extraordinary sand swimmer, the marsupial mole, is blind. This underground bulldozer relies on smell to find its prey. The lizards found here look and move like snakes, since legs are not very useful for sliding through sand.

On the sand waves and sand plains, spinifex made the explorers' journey more treacherous. It is a strange prickly grass, "like that on the seashore."

Where the clumps and rings of needle-sharp spines crowded too closely, the horses became trapped in a spiky maze. Sturt's animals would not touch it, and it seemed a useless, lifeless thing.

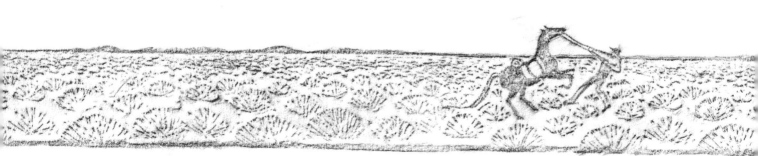

"The sharp points stuck into us at every step."

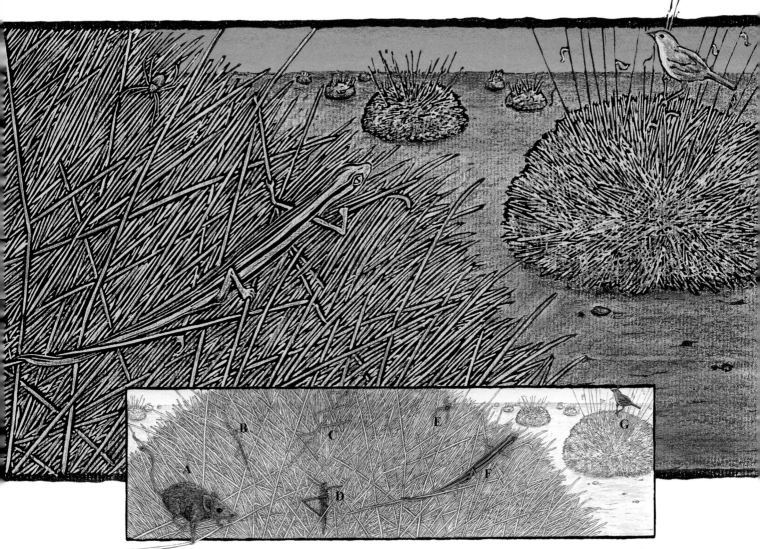

A Wongai ningaui
B Spinifex matchstick grasshopper
C Spinifex stick insect
D Spinifex katydid
E Grass spider
F Phasmid striped gecko
G Spinifexbird

But spinifex is a feast for termites. And termites are a feast for lizards and other animals. With its thickly matted spikes, spinifex also makes a perfect hideout.

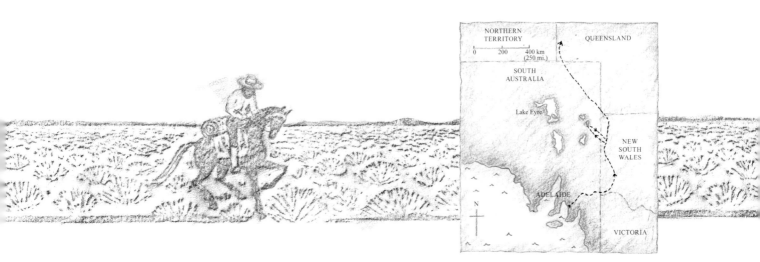

Perentie

When Sturt's party made its slow, painful way among the sand waves and spinifex, they found another obstacle. The clay pans between the sand waves were crisscrossed with cracks, like a giant jigsaw puzzle. In places, those cracks were deep and wide enough to break a horse's leg.

Although hazardous to Sturt and his team, these crevices offer protection to smaller creatures.

"A plain full of deep yawning rents and chasms six or seven feet in depth."

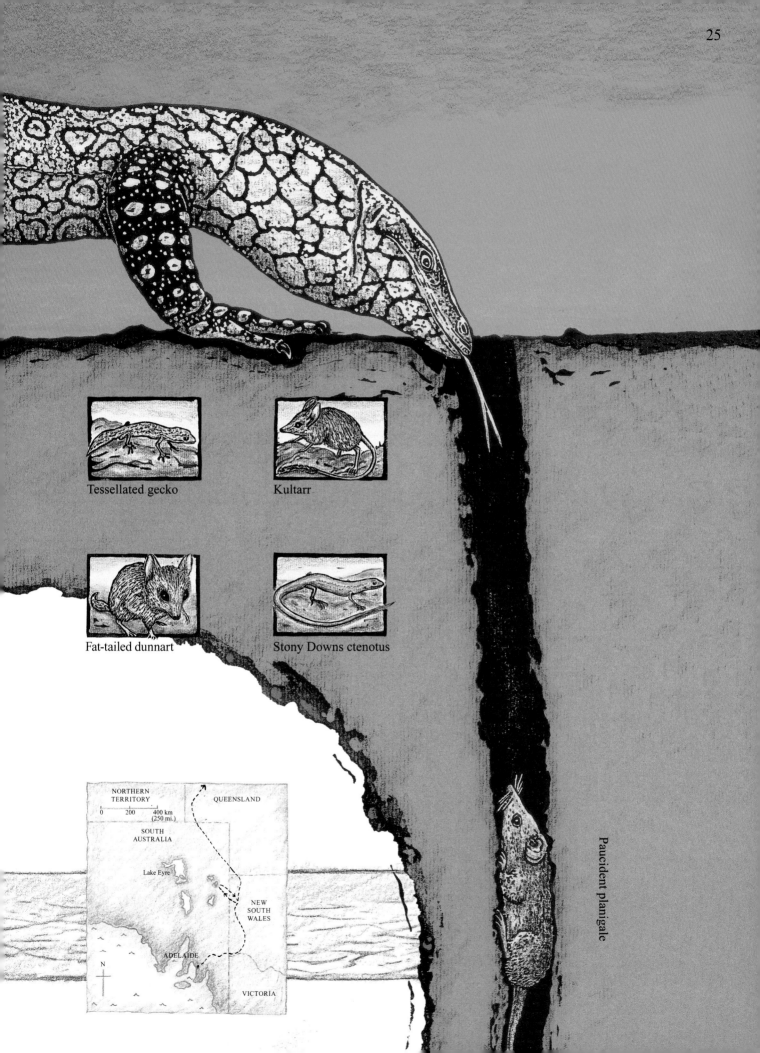

Tessellated gecko

Kultarr

Fat-tailed dunnart

Stony Downs ctenotus

Paucident planigale

NORTHERN
TERRITORY

QUEENSLAND

0   200   400 km
(250 mi.)

SOUTH
AUSTRALIA

Lake Eyre

NEW
SOUTH
WALES

ADELAIDE

N

VICTORIA

When night falls, many creatures leave these daytime dens.
It is time to hunt, and to beware of other hunters. Under the
cover of darkness, a night's work can be fast and ferocious.

"Did man ever see such a place?"

Left to right: katydid, stripe-faced dunnart eating a barking spider, kultarr, night parrot, kowari, scorpion, three-lined knob-tail, Hill's sheathtail-bat

The agile kowari (a rat-like marsupial) stalks and devours other mammals, while the knob-tailed gecko (a lizard) feasts on other geckos.

Despite the risks, the stripe-faced dunnart (a mouse-size marsupial) tackles almost anything, including venomous barking spiders and centipedes.

A Fat-tailed antechinus
(marsupial mouse)

B Dragon lizard

C Fossilized marine worm tracks
(made 500 million years ago)

D Bilby

E Fat-tailed dunnart

F Legless lizard

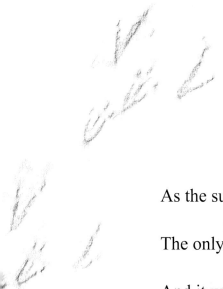

As the sun rises, the desert is still.

The only signs of the night hunters are patterns on the sand.

And it would take the skill of a true desert dweller to
follow those sandy traces and find the hunters now.

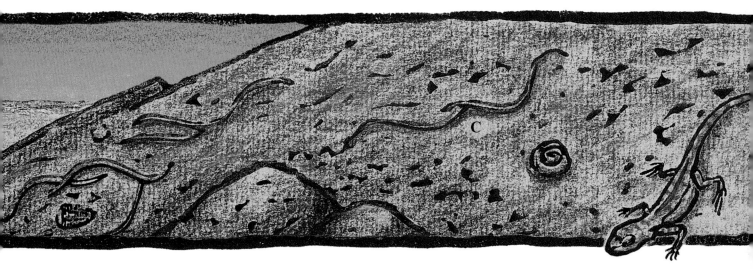

The sand tracks held little meaning for the European explorers.
They struggled home with stories of a lifeless, nightmare place.

To this day, many creatures of the desert remain a mystery,
and some have disappeared forever.

F

But this strange, dry wilderness continues to reveal an unexpected treasure—

the secret life of Australia's Dead Heart.

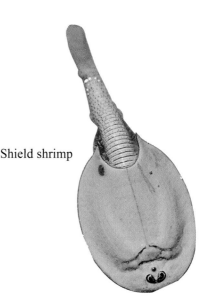

Shield shrimp

Thorny devil

Bibliography

Allen, G. and N. Cross, *Rainbowfishes of Australia and Papua New Guinea.* Sydney: Angus & Robertson, 1982.

Archer, M., S. Hand, and H. Godthelp, *Riversleigh.* Balgowlah, NSW: Reed, 1991.

Badman, F., B. Arnold, and S. Bell, eds., *A Natural History of the Lake Eyre Region,* illus. by P. Langdon. Port Augusta: National Parks and Wildlife Service's Northern Consultative Committee, 1991.

Baker, L. (comp.). *Mingkiri: A Natural History of Uluru by the Mutitjulu Community.* Alice Springs: Institute for Aboriginal Development Press, 1996.

Davey, K. *Our Arid Environment: Animals of Australia's Desert Regions.* Sydney: Reed, 1983.

Ehmann, H., *Encyclopedia of Australian Animals: Reptiles,* ed.: Ronald Strahan. Sydney: Angus & Robertson, 1992.

Isaacs, J. *Bush Food: Aboriginal Food and Herbal Medicine.* Sydney: Weldons, 1987.

Mascord, R. *Australian Spiders in Colour.* Sydney: Reed, 1970.

Quirk, S. and M. Archer, eds. *Prehistoric Animals of Australia.* Sydney: Australian Museum, 1983.

Rentz, D. *Grasshopper Country: The Abundant Orthopteroid Insects of Australia.* Sydney: University of New South Wales Press, 1996.

Rich, P., G. Van Tets, and F. Knight, *Kadimakara: Extinct Vertebrates of Australia.* Lilydale: Australian Pioneer Design Studio, 1985.

Robinson, M. *A Field Guide to Frogs of Australia.* Chatswood, NSW: Australian Museum/Reed, 1993.

Shepard, M. *The Simpson Desert: Natural History and Human Endeavour.* Adelaide: Royal Geographical Society of Australasia/ Giles, 1992.

Simpson, K., ed., *Field Guide to the Birds of Australia: The Most Complete One-Volume Book of Identification,* illus. by N. Day. Victoria: Viking O'Neil, 1993.

Stokes, E. *To the Inland Sea: Charles Sturt's Expedition 1844–45.* Melbourne: Hutchinson, 1986.

Strahan, R., ed. *The Australian Museum Complete Book of Australian Mammals.* Sydney: Angus & Robertson, 1993.

Sturt, C. *Journal of the Central Australian Expedition, 1844–5,* J. Waterhouse, ed. London: Caliban, 1984.

Swan, K. and M. Carnegie. *In Step with Sturt.* Melbourne: Graphic Books, 1979.

Triggs, B. *Tracks, Scats, and Other Traces: A Field Guide to Australian Mammals.* Melbourne: Oxford University Press, 1996.

Turner-Neale, M., J. Henderson, and S. Dobson. *Bush Foods: Arrernte Foods from Central Australia.* Alice Springs: Institute for Aboriginal Development Press, 1994.

Van Oosterzee, P. *The Centre: The Natural History of Australia's Desert Regions,* photos by R. Morrison. Sydney: Reed, 1991.

Vanderbeld, J. *Nature of Australia: A Portrait of the Island Continent.* Sydney: Collins/Australian Broadcasting Corporation, 1988.

Zborowski, P. *Animals in Disguise: A Journey into Nature's Deception.* Balgowlah, NSW: Reed, 1991.

Marsupial mole

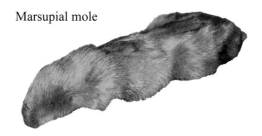

Gibber earless dragon

Robust duneslider

Kowari

A Note from the Author-Illustrator

Our family spent a number of weeks exploring some
remote areas in Central Australia, and I was intrigued
by the ironies inherent in the desert landscapes:
what seemed like empty sand dunes were covered
in animal tracks in the morning, while fossilized
marine creatures were embedded in the rock walls
of canyons. Further ironies became apparent when I
read explorer Charles Sturt's diary of his expedition
to find the inland sea in 1844–1845. He strangely
described desert features using water images —
"waves" of sand, spinifex like "seashore grass."

While keeping a focus on the wildlife of each
desertscape and using Sturt's journey to link these
places, I wanted to portray Central Australia through
its fascinating paradoxes. For example, the first
European explorers believed the deserts to be lifeless,
yet there is actually a great variety of hidden and
well-adapted wildlife. The intimate knowledge
of plants and animals of the desert developed by
indigenous groups had allowed them to survive
there for thousands of years and was ignored by
the explorers at their own peril. And a vast inland
sea once existed, but now there are only rolling sand
dunes and lakes of pavement stones. Ironically, Sturt
was right about the existence of an inland sea in
Central Australia — his expedition was only
14 million years too late!

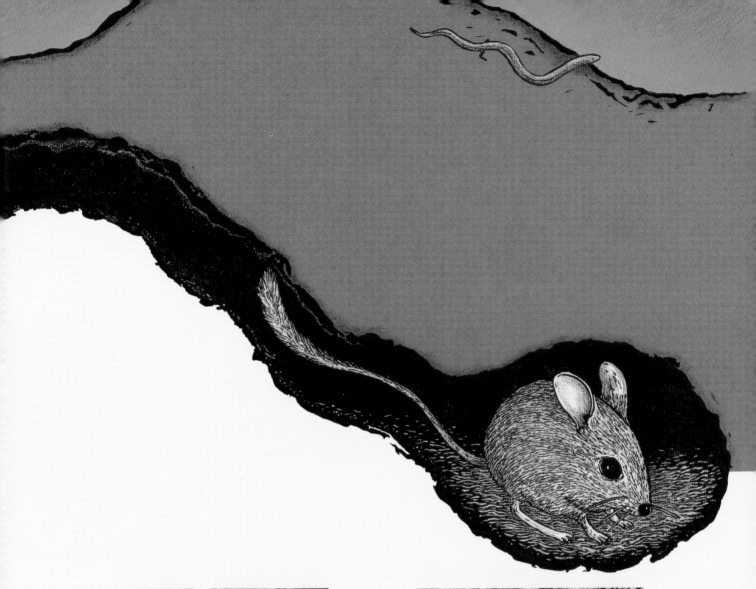

Narelle Oliver at border crossing

Mulga campsite, clothes, and camera

Desert dune animal tracks

Desert pavement stones

Acknowledgments

Many thanks to David Cox for expert advice on all things horse-related; Patrick Couper, Curator, Vertebrates, Queensland Museum; Phillip Lawless, Assistant Curator, Arachnology, Queensland Museum; Geoff Monteith, Senior Curator, Lower Entemology, Queensland Museum; Greg Rogers for design assistance; Steve Wilson, Reference Center Assistance, Queensland Museum; and the staff at the Charles Sturt Museum, Adelaide.

Photographs of the shield shrimp, thorny devil, and kowari on pages 32 and 33 courtesy of the Queensland Museum; photograph of the gibber earless dragon on page 33 courtesy of Pavel German and Nature Focus; photograph of the robust duneslider on page 33 courtesy of Harry Ehmann and Nature Focus; photograph of the marsupial mole on page 32 courtesy of D Roff and Nature Focus.

Quotes from Charles Sturt's diary come from the *Journal of the Central Australian Expedition, 1844–5*, edited by J. Waterhouse.

This project has been assisted by the Commonwealth Government through the Australia Council, its arts funding, and its advisory body.

For Greg